James Orchard Halliwell-Phillipps

The Metrical History of Tom Thumb the Little

As Issued Early in the Eighteenth Century, in Three Parts

James Orchard Halliwell-Phillipps

The Metrical History of Tom Thumb the Little
As Issued Early in the Eighteenth Century, in Three Parts

ISBN/EAN: 9783337203542

Printed in Europe, USA, Canada, Australia, Japan

Cover: Foto ©ninafisch / pixelio.de

More available books at **www.hansebooks.com**

The Impression of this Book is limited to Thirty Copies.

PRINTED FOR THE EDITOR
BY WHITTINGHAM AND WILKINS, AT THE
CHISWICK PRESS,
TOOKS COURT, CHANCERY LANE.

THE METRICAL HISTORY

OF

TOM THUMB THE LITTLE,

AS ISSUED EARLY IN THE

EIGHTEENTH CENTURY,

IN THREE PARTS.

EDITED BY
J. O. HALLIWELL, ESQ., F.R.S.

LONDON:
PRINTED FOR THE EDITOR.
1860.

PREFACE.

THE earliest notice of the popular history of Tom Thumb, as known in England, occurs in Scot's Discoverie of Witchcraft, 1584, where he speaks of it as amongst the tales used by servants to frighten children withall. Tom Thumb is there spoken of in company with " changlings, incubus, Robin Good-fellow, the spoorne, the mare, the man in the oke, the helle-waine, the fiere-drake, the puckle, hobgobblin, Tom Tumbler, boneles, and such other bugs," *bugs*, of course, meaning, bugbears. He is again mentioned in some verses prefixed to Coryat's Crudities, 1611—"Tom Thumbe is dumbe, untill the pudding creepe, in which he was intomb'd, then out doth peepe." This story of the pudding appears to have been the most popular in connection with him. It is once more alluded to in Ben Jonson's masque of the Fortunate Isles, where mention is made of "Thomas Thumb in a pudding fat, with Doctor Rat."

The first part of Tom Thumb, in its metrical form, was printed for John Wright in black-letter in 1630, and reprinted more than once for F. Coles. With slight alterations, this part continued to be reprinted for two centuries. About the year 1700, two other parts were added; and the three parts were continually reprinted in the eighteenth century. Notwithstanding, however, their great popularity, it is exceedingly difficult at the present day to meet with a complete copy of the three parts.

Preface. 7

Richard Johnson, in 1621, published a prose version of this penny history, in the preface to which he observes:—"The ancient tales of Tom Thumbe in the olde time have beene the only revivers of drouzy age at midnight; old and young have with his tales chim'd mattens till the cocks crow in the morning; batchelors and maides with his tales have compassed the Christmas fire-blocke till the curfew bell rings candle out; the old shepheard and the young plow-boy after their dayes labour have carold out a tale of Tom Thumbe to make them merry with; and who but little Tom hath made long nights seem short, and heavy toyles easie?" This prose story of Tom Thumb is the earliest copy yet discovered; but there can be no doubt that tracts on the subject were in circulation in England many years previously.

THE FIRST PART OF

THE LIFE OF TOM THUMB.

Of the Parentage, Birth & education of Tom Thumb, *with all the merry Pranks he played in his Childhood.*

IN Arthur's Court Tom Thumb did live
    A man of mickle might,
Who was the best of the Table Round,
    And eke a worthy Knight.

In stature but an inch in height,
    Or quarter of a span;
How think you this courageous Knight
    Was prov'd a valiant man.

His father was a ploughman plain,
   His mother milk'd the cow,
And yet the way to get a Son
   This couple knew not how.

Until the time the good old man
   To learned Merlin goes,
And there to him in deep distress,
   In secret manner shews,

How in his heart he'd wish to have
   A Child in time to come,
To be his heir, tho' it might be,
   No bigger than his thumb.

Of this old Merlin then foretold,
   How he his wish should have;
And so a son of stature small,
   This charmer to him gave.

No blood nor bones in him should be,
   His shape it being such,
That he should hear him speak, but not
   His wandering shadow touch.

Tom Thumb the Little.

But so unseen to overcome,
   Whereat it pleas'd him well,
Begat and born in half an hour,
   For to fit his father's will;

And in four minutes grew so fast,
   That he became so tall,
As was the ploughman's thumb in length
   And so she did him call.

Tom Thumb, the which the Fairy Queen,
   Did give him to his name,
Who with her train of gobblings grim
   Unto the christening came.

When they cloathed him so fine and gay
   In garments rich and fair;
The which did serve him many years
   In seemly sort to wear.

His hat made of an oaken leaf,
   His shirt a spider's webb,
Both light and soft for his small limbs,
   Which were so smally bred.

His hose and doublet thistle down,
  Together weav'd full fine;
And stockings of the apple green,
  Made of the outer rhine.

His garters were two little hairs,
  Pluck'd from his mother's eye;
His shoes made of a mouse's skin,
  And tann'd most curiosly.

Thus like a valiant Gallant he
  Does venture forth to go
With other children in the street,
  His pretty pranks to show;

Where for counters, pins, and points,
  And cherry stones did play,
Till he amongst the gamsters young,
  Lost all his stock away.

Yet he could not the same renew,
  When as most nimbly he
Would dive into the cherry bags,
  And there partaker be.

Unseen or felt by any one,
    Until a scholar shut
The nimble youth into a box
    Wherein his pins were put.

Of whom to be reveng'd he took,
    In mirth and pleasant game,
Black pots and glasses which he hung
    Upon a light sun-beam.

The other boys did do the same,
    In pieces tore them quite,
For which they were severely whipt,
    Which made him laugh outright.

So poor Tom Thumb restrained was,
    From this his sport and play;
And by his mother after that
    Compell'd at home to stay.

Whereas about Christmas time,
    His mother a hog had kill'd,
And Tom would see the pudding made,
    For fear it should be spoil'd.

*Of Tom's falling into the Pudding Bowl, and his
Escape out of the Tinker's Budget.*

HE sat the candle for to light,
 Upon the pudding bowl,
Of which there is unto this day,
 Some pretty stories told.

For Tom fell in, and could not be
 For some time after found,
For in the blood and batter he
 Was lost and almost drown'd.

But she not knowing of the same,
 Directly after that,
Into the pudding stir'd her son,
 Instead of mincing fat.

Now this pudding of the largest size,
 Into the kettle thrown,
Made all the rest to jump about,
 As with a whirlwind blown.

But so it tumbled up and down,
  Within the liquor there,
As if the devil had been boil'd,
  Such was the mother's fear.

That up she took the pudding strait,
  So gave it at the door
Unto a Tinker, which from thence
  He in his budget bore.

But as the Tinker climb'd a stile,
  He chanc'd to let a crack;
How! good old man, cry'd Tom Thumb
  Still hanging at his back.

Which made the Tinker for to run,
  And would no longer stay,
But cast both bag and pudding too
  Over the hedge away.

From whence poor Tom got loose at last,
  And home return'd again,
For he from great dangers long
  In safety did remain.

Untill such time his mother went
  For to milk her kine,
Where Tom unto a thistle fast,
  She linked with a line.

Of Tom Thumb being tied to a thistle; of his Mother's Cow eating him up; with his strange Deliverance out of the Cow's Belly.

A THREAD that held him to the same,
  For fear the blustering wind
Would blow him thence, so as she might
  Her son in safety find.

But mark the hap, a cow came by
  And up the Thistle eat:
Poor Tom withal, who as a dock,
  Was made the red cows meat.

But being mist his mother went
  Calling him every where;
Where art thou Tom? where art thou?
  Quoth he, here, mother, here.

In the red Cows Belly here,
    Your Son is swallow'd up;
All which within her fearful heart
    Much woeful cholar put.

Mean time the cow was troubled sore,
    In this her rumbling womb,
And could not rest until that she
    Had backwards cast Tom Thumb,

Now all besmeared as he was,
    His mother took him up,
And home to bear him hence, poor lad,
    She in her apron put.

Tom Thumb is carried away by a Raven, and swallowed up by a Giant; with several other strange accidents that befel him.

NOW after this, in sowing time
    His father would him have
Into the field to drive the plough,
    And therewithal him gave

A whip made of a barley straw,
    For to drive the cattle on;
There in a furrow'd land new sown,
    Poor Tom was lost and gone.

Now by a raven of great strength,
    Poor Tom away was born;
And carried in a carrion's beak,
    Just like a grain of corn.

Unto a giants castle top,
    Whereon he let him fall,
And soon the Giant swallowed up,
    His body, cloaths and all;

But in his Belly Tom Thumb did
    So great a rumbling make,
That neither night nor day he could
    The smallest quiet take.

Until the giant him had spew'd
    Full three miles in the sea;
There a large Fish soon took him up,
    And bore him hence away,

The lusty Fish was after caught,
    And to King Arthur sent,
Where Tom was kept, being a Dwarf,
    Until his time was spent.

Long time he liv'd in loyalty,
    Beloved of the Court,
And none like Tom was so esteem'd
    Amongst the better sort.

Tom Thumb by the Command of King Arthur dances a Galliard upon the Queen's left hand.

AMONG the deeds of courtship done,
    His Highness did command,
That he should dance a galliard brave
    Upon the Queen's left-hand.

All which he did, and for the same
    Our King his signet gave.
Which Tom about his middle wore
    Long time a girdle brave.

Behold it was a rich reward
   And given by the King,
Which to his Praise and worthiness
   Did lasting honour bring.

For while he lived in the court,
   His pleasant pranks were seen,
And he, according to Report
   Was favoured by the Queen.

Tom rides a hunting with the King.

NOW after that the King he would
   Abroad for Pleasure go,
Yet still Tom Thumb must be with him
Plac'd on his saddle bow.

But on a time when as it rain'd,
   Tom Thumb most nimbly crept,
Into his button-hole where he
   All in his bosom slept,

And being near his Highness heart,
   Did crave a wealthy boon;
A noble gift the which the King
   Commanded should be done.

For to relieve his father's wants,
   And mother's being old;
It was as much of silver coin
   As well his arms could hold.

So then away goes lusty Tom,
   With three-pence at his back:
A heavy burden which did make
   His very bones to crack.

So travelling two days and nights,
   In labour and great pain,
He came unto the house whereat
   His parents did remain;

Which was but half a mile in space,
   From good King Arthur's court,
All this in eight and forty hours
   He went in weary sort.

But coming to his father's door,
    He there such entrance had,
As made his parents both rejoice,
    For he thereat was glad.

So his mother in her apron put
    Her gentle son in haste.
And by the fire-side within,
    A walnut shell him plac'd,

And then they feasted him three days
    Upon a hazel nut,
On which he rioted long,
    And them to charges put:

And thereupon grew wonderous sick,
    In eating so much meat,
That was sufficient for a month
    For this great man to eat.

So when his business call'd him forth
    King Arthur's court to see,
From which no longer Tom it's said,
    Could now a stranger be;

But a few moist April drops,
   Which settled on the way,
His long and weary journey
   Did hinder and so stay,

Until his careful mother took
   A birding trunk in sport,
And with one blast blew this her son
   Into King Arthur's court.

Of Tom's running at Tilt; with other Exercises performed by him.

THUS he at tilt and tournaments
   Was entertained so,
That all the rest of Arthur's Knights
   Did him much pleasure show.

And good Sir Launcelot du Lake,
   Sir Tristram and Sir Guy,
Yet none compar'd to brave Tom Thumb
   In acts of cavalry.

In honour of which noble day,
    And for his lady's sake,
A challenge in King Arthur's court,
    Tom Thumb did bravely make.

'Gainst whom these noble Knights run,
    Sir Khion and the rest;
But yet Tom Thumb with all his might,
    Did bear away the best.

At last Sir Launcelot du Lake,
    In manly sort came in,
And with this stout and hardy Knight
    A Battle did begin.

Which made the courtiers all aghast,
    For there this valiant man,
Thro' Launcelot's steed before them all
    With nimble manner ran:

Yea horse and all, with spear and Shield
    As hardly e'er was seen,
But only by King Arthur's self,
    And his beloved Queen.

Who from her Finger took a ring,
    Thro' which Tom did make way,
Not touching it in simple sort,
    As it had been in play.

He also cleft the smallest hair
    From the fair lady's head,
From hurting her whose even hand
    Him lasting Honours bred.

Such were his deeds and noble Acts,
    In Arthur's court were shewn,
The like in all the world beside,
    Before was never known.

Tom is taken sick and dies.

THUS at his sports Tom toil'd himself,
    That he a sickness took,
Thro' all which manly exercise
    His Strength had him forsook

Where lying on his bed sore sick
    King Arthur's Doctors came,
By cunning skill and physick's art,
    To ease and cure the same,

He being both slender and tall,
    The cunning doctors took
A fine perspective glass thro' which
    They took a careful look,

Into his sickly body down,
    And therein saw that death
Stood ready in his wasted Guts,
    To seize his vital Breath.

His arms and legs consum'd as small,
    As was a spider's web,
Thro' which his dying hours grew,
    And all his Limbs were dead.

His face no bigger than an ant's
    Which hardly could be seen,
The Loss of this renowned Knight
    Much griev'd the King and Queen.

And so with grief and quietness
    He left the earth below,
And up into the Fairy Land
    His fading Ghost did go.

Where the Fairy Queen receiv'd
    With heavy mournful chear,
The body of this valiant Knight,
    Whom she esteem'd so dear.

For with her flying nymphs in green,
    She took him from his bed,
With musick sweet and melody,
    As soon as Life was fled.

For whom King Arthur and his Knights
    Full forty days did mourn;
In the remembrance of his name,
    That strangely thus was born.

He built a tomb of marble grey,
    And year by year did come,
To celebrate the mournful day,
    And burial of Tom Thumb.

Whose fame lives here in England still,
   Amongst the country sort,
Of whom the wives and Children dear
   Tell pretty tales in sport.

But here's a wonder come at last,
   Which some will scarce believe,
After two hundred years were past,
   He did new life receive.

The Fairy Queen she lov'd him so,
   As you shall understand,
That once again she let him go,
   Down from the Fairy Land.

The very time that he return'd
   Unto the Court again,
It was, as we are well assur'd,
   In good King Arthur's reign.

Where in the presence of the King,
   He many wonders wrought,
Recited in the second part,
   Which now is to be bought

In Irongate, in Derby Town;
   Where are sold fine Histories many,
And pleasant tales e'er was told,
   For purchase of One Penny.

THE SECOND PART OF

THE LIFE OF TOM THUMB.

Of Tom's Return from Fairy Land; he falls into the Firmity; and of the sad Misfortunes that attended him.

WHEN good King Arthur he did reign,
    With all his Knights about him,
Tom Thumb he then did entertain,
    For he could not do without him.

Behold he made right pretty sport,
    Which pleased passing well;
And therefore in King Arthur's court
    He was allow'd to dwell.

His Parents were of small account,
    And he was small of growth,
Yet they on Fortune's Wing's did fly,
    She did befriend them both.

For many long and pleasant years
    He was belov'd by all.
The royal court, both prince and peers,
    Wept to see his funeral.

The longest Time will ended be,
    So was Tom's life at last;
The mourning court did weep to see
    His breath was but a blast:

So mounting to the Fairy Queen,
    She did her love express,
By giving him a robe of green,
    A sweet and comely dress.

In the Elesian shades he reign'd
    Two hundred years and more,
So by the Queen it was ordain'd,
    That he her scepter bore;

As King of all the Fairy Land,
    And had continued still,
But that as you may understand,
    It was her gracious will,

To send him to the lower world,
   In triumph once again;
So with a puff or blast him hurl'd
   Down with a mighty pain;

With mighty force it happened he
   Did fall, as some report
Into a pan of firmity
   In good King Arthur's court.

The cook that bore it then along,
   Was struck with a surprise,
For with the fall the firmity
   Flew up into his eyes.

The cook was running on full tilt,
   When Tom fell from the air;
The pan of firmity was spilt,
   O what a sight was there!

The cook was frighted to the heart,
   Tom Thumb he sprawling lay;
No one was there to take his part,
   Alack and a well-a-day.

His coat of green was then besmear'd
   With firmity all o'er;
Likewise another death he fear'd,
   His bones were sore all o'er.

He got out of the firmity
   As well as he was able,
They dragged him immediately
   Before King Arthur's table;

Where he in pomp at dinner sat,
   With wine and music sweet,
For many noble Knights were met
   To taste a royal treat,

With clubs and staves, forks and prongs,
   He guarded was unpitied,
To answer for the mighty Wrongs
   Which he had there committed.

Now as they enter'd in the Hall,
   With Tom that little sprite,
O how the multitude did bawl,
   To shew their hateful spite.

Some said he was a Fairy Elf,
    And therefore did deserve to die;
But Tom secur'd himself,
    As you'll find by and by.

For just as they began to vote
    What Death he should endure,
He jumped down a Miller's throat,
    And there he lay secure,

Not one of all the multitude
    Perceiv'd the Way he went;
Thus tho' his Death they then pursu'd,
    Tom did the same prevent,

They look'd about, but could not find
    Tom Thumb in any Place;
Wherefore like men perplex'd in Mind,
    Each suffered sad disgrace.

*Tom torments a Miller while he lays in his Paunch;
and of other wonderful Things that happened.*

THEN did the multitude depart,
    Like dogs that burnt their Tails,
Each being vexed to the heart,
O how they gnaw'd their nails,

To think they had their prisoner lost
    In presence of the King;
Never was man so strangely crost,
    It was a grievous thing.

The Miller too above the rest,
    He scowered like a ferrit:
Still crying out he was possest
    With some familiar Spirit.

Tom often pinch'd him by the tripes,
    And made the Miller roar,
Alas! alas! ten thousand stripes
    Could not have vex'd him more.

Ah! wo is me, the Miller cry'd,
  Good-lack, good-lack a-day;
Some spiteful imp does in me bide
  Which does the antick play.

For help he to the doctor sought,
  Being distracted nigh;
But the Miller little thought
  Poor Tom was in his Belly.

When he before the Doctor came;
  And told him every thing
Which he had suffered, Tom by name
  Did whistle, dance, and sing.

The Doctor he was thunder struck,
  To think what he should be;
I fear said he, some evil lurks,
  Sure Satan speaks in thee.

You lie, quoth Tom, and then he sung
  A short but pleasant song,
Your latin and your lying tongue
  Does many people wrong.

I was a courtier, 'tis well known,
    Two hundred years ago,
When good King Arthur had the crown
    As thousands then did know.

And am I called a Devil now,
    Who never did no harm,
I solemly protest and vow,
    I'll be reveng'd on you.

The Doctor then affrighted was,
    Worse than he was before,
And sent for twenty learned men
    The Miller to restore.

So being come into the hall,
    Strait to their great surprise,
Tom for a cup of sack did call,
    And musick too likewise,

The miller being fast asleep,
    And sitting in his chair,
All people strait began to weep,
    When they his voice did hear.

With much ado they rous'd him then,
   So on his feet he stood.
For they were understanding men,
   Who came to do him good.

By turns they strait examined him,
   How he is life did square,
For they were certain that a limb
   Of Lucifer was there.

Says one, I am persuaded you
   Have often play'd the thief,
In taking more than was your due,
   Which causes all your grief.

So then the Miller did confess
   What he had said was true,
Yet all my friends, nevertheless,
   My father did so too;

And eke my grandsire, who in mould
   Is sleeping now full low,
For he this very Mill did hold
   One hundred years ago:

If they did so, why may not I
    One bushel take of two?
Tom Thumb cry'd out immediately,
    A hopeful thievish crew,

You must leave off they all did cry,
    Steal not in time to come,
A voice immediately reply'd,
    Why don't you know Tom Thumb?

So said, they all began to run,
    In a distracted case,
And left the Miller all alone,
    Who in a little space,

Ran to a mighty river side,
    To ease his body there,
And turn'd Tom Thumb into the tide,
    Who swam I know not where;

But as the ancient writers say,
    Near to the Northern Pole,
Where many a lusty salmon lay,
    Who swallowed him up whole.

Tom being swallowed up by a Salmon, is caught by a Fishman; and of the Sport he made in the Fish's Belly.

 A FISHERMAN came out of Rye,
    With nets and other geer;
The seas were rough, the winds were high,
    Yet he his course did steer.

'Midst foaming billows that did roar,
    Until he came at last,
Where he had fish'd not long before
    And there his net he cast,

And drew it up with great success,
    Which made the fishman laugh,
Having as near as he could guess,
    One dozen at a draught,

Unto his net so fast they throng,
    Which did them much surprise,
For some of them was large and long,
    Others of a smaller size.

At length as I the truth may tell,
   He with that salmon met,
Which had gotten poor Tom Thumb,
   And almost broke his net.

Says he, I never in my life
   Had such a one before;
I'll home to honest Joan my wife,
   And let her know my store.

So having stow'd them in his boat,
   He home began to steer,
Singing a sweet and pleasant note
   For this his happy cheer.

So near the pleasant town of Rye,
   His freighted boat was blow'd,
Blyth Joan she came immediately
   And smil'd to see the load.

His fish up to the market place,
   They brought in state and pride;
But O the salmon was the best
   Of all the fish beside.

The people flocked far and near,
 To buy some fish of him,
Because he had, as did appear,
 As good as e'er did swim.

Amongst the rest a steward came,
 Who would the salmon buy,
And other fish that he did name,
 But he would not comply.

The steward said, are you so proud,
 If so, I'll not by any;
So then bespoke Tom Thumb aloud,
 Sir, give the other penny.

At this they all began to stare,
 To hear his sudden joke,
Nay, some was frighted to the heart,
 And thought the dead fish spoke.

It was a strange and sudden touch,
 So the Fisherman and they
Who heard him speak, wondered much,
 And had no more to say.

As they were standing in amaze,
    At what they then had heard,
Tom again his voice did raise,
    And spoke with good regard;

Saying, the like in all the Land
    Before was never seen;
Present this Salmon out of hand
    Unto the King and Queen.

So the steward made no more ado,
    But bid a penny more;
Because he said he never knew
    A fish to speak before:

So the steward's Master by report,
    Was made a noble Lord;
He sent the Salmon to the court
    In hopes of a great reward.

Having a worthy present
    To make the Lord amends,
The King returns a compliment,
    And so the chapter ends.

Which fairly leads us to the next,
    The compliment was poor;
The noble Lord was sorely vex'd,
    To find he had no more.

The King's Cook sticks a Fork in Tom's Breech, and carries him to the King; and of his happy Deliverance.

TWO noble Knights a wager laid,
    About I know not what;
Some say they at a fencing play'd,
    And some assure us not.

Some say it was a game at bowls,
    One morning in the forest;
Tho' both of them were honest Men,
    The same was won and lost.

The court was full of wagers then,
    Some laid an hundred pound;
Dukes, lords, and worthy gentlemen,
    Much sport and pastime found.

The King it seems amongst the rest,
    A noble dinner lost;
The salmon then was to be drest,
    Which so much money cost.

The cook was then to dress the same,
    And then by chance he saw
The little man *Tom Thumb* by name,
    Within the salmon's maw.

He started strait, and said, Alas!
    How came this fellow here?
Strange things I find are brought to pass,
    He shall not now get clear,

Because he vow'd to go thro' stitch,
    And him to Justice bring,
He stuck a fork into his breech,
    And bore him to the King.

Who being then at council board,
    About some state affairs,
He could not very well afford
    To lay aside his cares

For such a slender cause as this,
   Wherefore as many say,
He did the busy Cook dismiss
   Until another day.

So the Cook it seems, did bear in mind,
   His old supposed wrong.
Therefore poor Tom must be confin'd
   Close in a prison strong.

But ne'er a prison was secure,
   When others were asleep,
For little Tom they might be sure
   He'd thro' the key-hole creep.

Therefore they bound him hand and foot
   So cruel was his fate;
And in a mouse-trap he was put
   To peep between the grate.

Alas! he made lamentable moan,
   And oft would sigh and say,
Because that he was all alone,
   Alack and well-a-day.

He labour'd, but could not get loose,
  By all that he could do,
The mouse-trap wires were so close,
  Poor Tom could not get thro'.

When he had lain a week or more,
  Bathed in melting tears,
Under a guard he came before
  The King and all his peers.

Poor Tom was in a piteous trim,
  And seem'd to blush for shame,
The Lords and Knights requir'd him
  To tell from whence he came.

Now it may please your Majesty,
  Our prisoner reply'd,
I will rehearse my pedigree,
  Nothing shall be deny'd.

And thereupon he did report
  The manner of his Birth,
And how in good King Arthur's court
  He lived till his death.

Tom Thumb they call'd me in those days,
    As you shall understand;
Lords, Dukes, and Earls did speak my praise,
    And Princes of the land.

They gave him then a smiling look,
    And pardon'd him also,
Declaring they had read his book
    Many long years ago.

Tom Thumb the King did entertain,
    That he new sport might make,
And therefore Knighted him again
    For good King Arthur's sake.

Thus Tom in favour grew,
    Having all these things told,
The King believing it was true,
    Gave him a ring of gold.

Tom Thumb the Little.

Tom rides a Hunting with the King on a Mouse; a Farmer's Cat takes them both in her Mouth, and runs to the Top of a Tree with them.

TOM'S troubles being at an end,
    Now without any more ado,
Our King did for a Taylor send,
For to cloath him anew.

All enemies were vanish'd quite,
    That look'd so fierce and grim:
Now he appear'd a worthy Knight,
    They were in Love with him.

The manner of his worthy dress,
    In brief I will relate,
And then I think you needs must guess,
    How this little man was great.

His shirt was cut out of the wings
    Of a fair butterfly,
His breeches, coat, and other things
    All pleasing to the eye:

Upon his legs likewise he had
    Boots made of chicken leather,
Like any jolly noble lad
    He wore his hat and feather.

A taylor's needle was his sword,
    His head-piece was a thimble,
And when he fought, upon my word
    He made the giants tremble.

Now he was accosted thus,
    His Majesty reply'd,
Tom, will you take a course with us,
    We shall a hunting ride,

Together with the greatest part
    Of Nobles of our court?
Yes, yes, quoth Tom with all my heart,
    I ever lov'd such sport.

The King with many Noblemen
    Did gloriously appear,
For having put his Courtiers then
    To chace the nimble deer.

But poor Tom was at a loss,
   His nimble limbs they were so small,
For he was loath to ride a horse,
   For fear that he should fall.

A little mouse they did provide,
   And set him on the same,
O then he did in safety ride,
   As he pursu'd the game.

The King and his Nobility,
   As they did ride with speed,
They could not chuse but laugh to see
   Tom's little prancing steed.

They rode like Nobles of renown,
   Thro' many a park and plain,
And just before the sun set down,
   Each homeward turn'd again.

But coming near a farmer's house,
   Just by a forest side,
A cat jump'd out and caught the mouse
   Whereon Tom Thumb did ride.

She took him up between her jaws,
    And scower'd up a tree,
And as she scratch'd him with her claws,
    He cry'd out, Wo is me!

He laid his hand upon his sword,
    And run her thro' and thro';
And he for fear of falling roar'd,
    Puss likewise cry'd out mew.

It was a sad and bloody fight
    Between the Cat and he;
Puss valu'd not this worthy Knight,
    But scratch'd him bitterly.

The King and all his noble Peers,
    Were overcome with grief;
They heard his cries and saw his tears,
    But could not yield relief.

But at the length she let him drop,
    And they by meer good hap,
As he did tumble from the top,
    Did catch him in a cap.

His coat was tatter'd like a rag,
  And he look'd like a moam;
They put him in a hawking bag,
  And so they brought him home,

But Puss had claw'd and scratch'd him so
  Making his veins to bleed,
That he could neither stand nor go,
  But took his bed with speed;

Where many dying groans he sent
  Up to the Fairy Queen,
Alas, his tears of discontent
  By her were fairly seen.

She griev'd to see him how he lay,
  And sent a glorious train
Of little Fairies to convey
  Him to her court again.

The Fairy Queen, finding his Troubles, sends for him to Court, where he now remains.

BOTH far and near the tidings flew
    Of Tom's unhappy Fate;
And learned Doctors came to view
    His present dying state.

Not one of them could do him good,
    Or keep him safe from death;
For by their skill they understood
    He'd die for want of breath.

Within a Box of ivory,
    They made a downy bed,
The King and Nobles wept to see
    His life was almost fled.

Young virgins watch'd to keep him warm
    For six or seven nights,
At length appear'd a mighty swarm
    Of pretty Fairy Sprites;

With mourning garlands on their heads,
   His bed they compass'd round,
And folding down the Coverlid,
   Sir Tom Thumb there they found.

How he was bruis'd in every limb,
   Which wrought his life's decay;
And having all saluted him,
   Without the least delay,

They put him in a winding-sheet,
   More white than Lillies fair,
These Fairies all with music sweet,
   Did mount the lofty air.

And soon they vanish'd out of sight,
   Up to the Fairy Queen,
And from this time the worthy Knight
   Was never after seen.

The virgins posted to the King,
   With tears of discontent,
And having told him every thing,
   The court in mourning went.

And to his memory they built,
   A monument of Gold,
Upon King Edgar's dagger hilt,
   Most glorious to behold.

His worthy deeds recorded are,
   That ages yet to come,
May to their children young declare
   The deeds of brave Tom Thumb.

And pass away each winter's night,
   By a good Fire side,
With tales of mirth and much delight,
   At every Christmas tide.

Altho' a second time he's gone,
   Unto the gloomy shade:
Yet after that his life was fled,
   He many a Frolick play'd.

Amongst the Nobles of the court,
   Tho' in another Age,
Affording them delightful sport,
   And was King Thunstan's Page.

As you may read in Part the Third,
    And Fancy satisfy;
For loving friends, upon my word,
    Altho' he seem'd to die;

Death's fatal arrows prov'd in vain,
    As you shall understand,
For he was hurried back again,
    Down from the Fairy Land.

END OF THE SECOND PART.

THE THIRD PART OF

THE LIFE OF TOM THUMB.

In what strange Manner Tom Thumb came back a Third Time, and unfortunately fell into a Close-Stool.

IN woeful manner Tom thus left
    The King and all his Court,
Of all their Mirth they were bereft,
    He yielded them such Sport.

Unto his Memory was paid,
    For all his actions past,
Another monument was made,
    That should for ever last.

Now in the Elesian Fields he reigns
    King of the Fairy Land,
Where he the love of all obtains
    Ready at his command.

He to the Fairy Queen relates
    His mighty acts below,
His wonderful adventures great,
    As Edgar's court did shew.

In joyful sort he reign'd above,
    As he had done before,
The Fairy Queen to shew her love,
    Again he her scepter bore:

Until such time it pleas'd her that
    She'd send him once again,
And as all histories do agree,
    It was in Thunston's reign.

She cloathed him all o'er in green,
    And without more delay,
But with her great majestic mein,
    She hurry'd him away.

Where he descended thro' the air,
    This poor unhappy man,
By sad mishap, as you shall hear
    Fell in a close-stool pan.

So all besmear'd in piteous wise,
    Poor Tom was almost drown'd;
For in the filth he could not rise,
    Or scarce be ever found.

He then did cry, ah! wo is me,
    My misery don't decay;
Which caus'd the men to flee away,
    'Twas death, they could not stay.

Then all the people thronged fast,
    Such miracles to see,
There was he almost spent at last,
    For none durst set him free.

But he at last delivered was,
    When thousands did resort,
Brought in this piteous woeful case
    Unto King Thunston's court.

*Tom is brought before the King, with an Account
of his Actions.*

IN shameful sort Tom Thumb appear'd
    Before his Majesty,
But grown so weak, could not be heard,
    Which caus'd his malady.

All that beheld him stood amaz'd,
    And knew not what to say;
Some did endeavour him to seize,
    'Fore life did quite decay.

The doctor then with speed was call'd,
    His vitals to restore,
For in the excrement thus maul'd,
    He did their help implore.

That if his Majesty would grant,
    He would in humble sort
Declare the cause of all their want
    Of knowledge of the court.

At length the King resolved was,
    For to grant him his request,
And from his presence he should pass,
    For to ease himself and rest.

And that the doctor should take care
    For to bring him on demand;
So they Tom Thumb away did bear,
    For to wait the King's command.

The doctor thought to let him blood,
    But some did him oppose;
Others said it was not good,
    And a dispute arose.

Till one, a grave experienc'd man,
    Did all they say disanul,
For if his vessels they could scan,
    There's not a thimble full.

At last upon a learn'd debate,
    It was resolv'd by all,
How they would trust his life to fate,
    And wait his rise or fall.

But fortune proved yet his friend,
    As his life shews before;
Altho' she left him in the end,
    His miseries to deplore.

For at the last he rais'd his Head,
    In presence of them all,
And cry'd my life is not yet fled,
    My spirits I recal.

That I may answer for the wrong
    Which now is done to me;
And clear myself e'er it be long,
    Before his Majesty.

His speech did cause a great surprise,
    They knew not what to say,
For on a sudden Tom did rise,
    At which they fled away.

But his poor guardian trembling stood,
    Betwixt great hope and fear,
But Tom cry'd in a merry mood,
    Unto the King we'll steer.

His trial at the last drew near,
    Great preparations made,
For the King and Nobles stood in fear,
    Yet seemed not dismay'd:

For by his Majesty's command
    Poor Tom Thumb must appear,
For to answer such questions, and
    How he himself should clear.

When to their presence he was brought,
    He did amaze the court,
He paid obeysance where he thought
    Fit to yield them sport.

So the King ask'd him whence he came,
    The way he liv'd, and where,
He also then requires his name,
    Who caus'd this pannick fear.

Tom then relates his Actions past,
    How he had liv'd before,
And the reason of his being cast
    Down to the earth once more.

All that of them he did implore,
  To search the records past;
How sumptuously he was before,
  None might his memory blast.

For deeds renowned I was fam'd
  Now in oblivion lost,
Sir Tom Thomb I then was nam'd,
  Tho' fame my life hath crossed.

The which the King no sooner heard,
  But from his throne did rise,
And said, Sir Tom Thomb, for thy fame,
  None can thee equalize.

Thy birth, thy parentage is known,
  Traditions do make clear,
All people do you great renown
  In joyful memory bear.

So that from hence you need not fear,
  My favour you shall have.
To me your memory is dear,
  Henceforth you need not crave

For lodgings—Now the King resolv'd
    A palace should be fram'd,
The walls of this most stately place
    Were lovely to behold.

For workmanship it was a plan,
    Like gold that had been try'd,
The height thereof was but a span,
    And doors but one inch wide.

The inward parts were all japan,
    Which was for him so neat,
The workmanship so fine thereon,
    Nothing was more compleat.

That Tom now lives in pleasant sort,
    Who was belov'd of all.
He yielded them much mirth and sport,
    All waited on his call.

The King did him admire so,
    The wonder of the age,
His bounty farther to bestow,
    Thunston made him his page.

Tom Thumb the Little.

Tom grows in favour with the King, who buys him a Coach drawn by six Mice.

ALL troubles now are vanished,
    In peace Tom Thomb did live,
    No cares disturb his peace by night,
No miseries survive.

The greatest Storms will have an end,
    When calm succeeds again,
Fortune her bounty now did lend,
    And eas'd him of all pain.

All recreation thought could have,
    Or life could e'er afford,
All earthly joys that he could crave
    At his desire or word.

No mirth without him now might please,
    All to him did resort;
So he did live in splendid ease,
    Beloved by the court,

So that the King so pleased was,
    As for his ease and sake,
Thro' his dominions he might pass,
    Or recreation take.

Of smallest mice that might be found,
    For to draw his Coach appears,
Such stately steeds his wish did crown,
    Long tails with cropped ears.

So he enjoys his whole desire,
    Forgets his miseries past,
Ambition makes him still aspire,
    Which fatal proves at last.

For his desires were lustful grown
    Against her Majesty,
Finding of her one day alone,
    Which prov'd his tragedy.

Tom Thumb the Little.

Tom attempts to ravish the Queen.

SOME sacred solitary thought
    Had now possess'd the Queen,
She for some pleasant harbour sought,
    Both pleasant and serene.

Which having found, she laid her down,
    In hopes to ease her mind;
With soft repose her cares to drown,
    Nought seem'd to prove unkind.

Now with the thoughts that did molest
    Her breast, she laid her head
Upon the flowers in hopes of rest,
    Her anxious cares were fled.

For pleasant and delightful dreams,
    Did all her sorrows drown;
The God of Sleep his image frames,
    No power on her might frown,

Unknown or seen by any one,
   Tom Thumb observ'd the Queen,
And thus perceiving her alone,
   There he lay hid unseen.

A snail out of her shell did come,
   For to seek food and air,
Which being marked by Tom Thumb,
   He takes possession there;

Where for a time he lay conceal'd,
   Seen by no mortal eye,
From out of which he does creep out,
   A wonderous prodigy.

Where, unto his lavish'd view,
   The Queen was left alone,
His lustful thoughts now to pursue,
   He was resolved on.

His resolution then he arms,
   Resolved to pursue,
He some short time beheld her charms,
   Which did his flame renew.

But now approaching to the place
   Of his desired haven,
Not fearing the least disgrace,
   By eagerness was driven.

But all his hopes were vanquish'd quite,
   The Queen surpriz'd awoke
In great confusion and affright,
   At length these words she spoke,

What villain dare invade my rest,
   Or rob me of repose?
Of which Tom Thumb makes but a jest,
   And laughed as he rose.

The Queen with rage and fury fir'd,
   To see herself abus'd,
That of the King she then desir'd,
   Tom Thumb might be accus'd.

That nothing would her wrath appease,
   To free her from all strife,
Or set her mind at perfect ease,
   Until she had his life.

*Of Tom's Escape on a Butter-Fly, and the Manner
in which he was taken Prisoner.*

NOW all the court stood in amaze,
    To hear the Queen relate,
For some did Tom's fam'd actions praise,
    While others urg'd his fate.

After debates they did agree
    How he should there appear;
But their designs Tom did foresee,
    Which caus'd his pannick fear.

Perceiving now a mighty throng,
    Approaching near the place,
Ready to seize him, but e'er long,
    Retir'd with nimble pace.

Into his shell, where safe he lay,
    And unperceiv'd by all,
And made them search in vain all day,
    Such as design'd his fall.

But finding all retir'd and gone,
　　His anger to suffice,
In cautious sort he moves along,
　　Nature wants some Supplies.

But all in vain, no food he finds,
　　His joys are turn'd to grief,
Fortune that once seem'd to be kind,
　　Now yields him no relief.

So long he wandered, but in vain,
　　No Prospect yet appears,
Which did involve him in such Pain,
　　As captivates his fears,

At last with grief he laid him down,
　　His miseries to deplore,
For no expedient was found,
　　For to gain nature's Store.

At last a Butterfly he espy'd,
　　The which he seized in haste,
Upon his back he got astride,
　　With care himself he placed.

So with expanded wings she mounts,
    For he was plac'd secure,
His tender limbs lay all so soft,
    No hardships could endure.

As Providence ordained all things,
    To each one his own nature;
Tom's steed from tree to tree still climbs,
    His miseries were greater.

From Post to Pillar now he's tost,
    Again upon the ground,
And now aloft thus was he crost,
    No respite could be found.

But mark his fate, Tom's winged steed
    Did now direct his course,
As if by chance of fate decreed,
    With all his might and force

Unto the court, and hovering round,
    A banquet was prepared;
Where all in joy they do abound,
    No other sound was heard.

But in the middle of the sport
    Tom Thumb they did espy,
How he was riding round the court
    Upon a Butterfly.

The which in vain they strove to seize,
    Till his unhappy lot,
As on him stedfastly they gaze,
    He fell in a white Pot.

When searching long, at last they found,
    Tom in a piteous case;
He with the fall was almost drown'd,
    Such was his sad disgrace:

But not regarding of the moan,
    Away they did him bring,
Where for his crimes he must attone,
    Before the Queen and King.

Of Tom's being brought before the King, with his Behaviour during the Time of his Trial.

AT last the mournful day is come,
    In which Tom must appear
Before the King to have his doom,
    His plaint no more would hear.

For their Aversion was so great,
    None would plead his cause,
But rather usher'd on his fate,
    To gain the Queen's applause.

Unto all they said, this little man
    Made no reply at all,
For fear his words they should trapan,
    Which rais'd their spleen and gall.

Unto all which the King did swear,
    By all his pomp and power,
That if himself he did not clear,
    He should be hang'd that hour.

So he did raise his little head,
    And said, ah, woe is me,
My vital spirits are just fled,
    So pass your last decree.

For here no respite can I find,
    But one continual strife.
Exert your power, glut your mind,
    And take my wretched life.

This valiant answer mov'd the court,
    All but the angry Queen,
Her rage and fury did transport,
    No one could intervene.

Some pleaded hard that they would give
    Him present Punishment,
Unto some more remoter place,
    Should be his banishment.

But still in vain, they would not hear,
    No pity should be shown,
Since for the fact he must pay dear,
    His life must it atone.

So the King his sentence he declar'd,
    How hanged he should be,
And that a Gibbet should be rear'd,
    And none should set him free.

After his sentence thus was past,
    Unto a Prison he was led,
So in a Mouse-trap they made him fast,
    He had no other bed.

His tender limbs not us'd to such,
    Did bruise in piteous wise,
In his past life he suffered much,
    Yet none regards his cries.

His liberty now to regain,
    His Prison strives to break,
Where long he laboured with great pains
    His life was now at stake.

Nothing but death appears in view,
    Which did his thoughts employ,
Yet for no Pardon would he sue,
    No life again enjoy.

Tom thus secur'd, was left alone,
    For death he does prepare,
In piteous sort he makes his moan,
    Being driven to despair.

At last by chance a cat him spy'd,
    And for a mouse did take,
She him attacked on each side,
    And did his Prison break.

Tom in endeavouring to make his Escape falls into a Spider's Web; and of his unexpected Death.

THE cat perceiving her mistake,
    Away she fled with speed,
Which made poor Tom to flight betake,
    Being thus from Prison freed.

Resolving there no more to dwell,
    But break the King's decree,
Into a spider's web he fell,
    And could not thence get free.

The spider watching for his Prey,
　　Tom took to be a fly,
And seized him without delay,
　　Regarding not his cry.

The blood out of his body drains,
　　He yielded up his breath;
Thus he was freed from all Pains,
　　By his unlook'd for death.

Thus you have heard his actions all,
　　Likewise his actions great,
His Rise, his Progress, and his fall,
　　Thus ushered in by fate.

Although he's dead, his Memory lives,
　　Recorded ever sure;
His very name, some pleasure gives,
　　And ever will endure.

FINIS.

www.ingramcontent.com/pod-product-compliance
Lightning Source LLC
Chambersburg PA
CBHW020225090426
42735CB00010B/1592